BIGIDEA'S VeggieTales®

HEROES OF THE BIBLE

BIG IDEA®

VeggieTales® is a registered trademark of Big Idea Productions, Inc.
© 2003 Big Idea Productions, Inc. All rights reserved. Used with permission.

® **Dalmatian Press, LLC, 2003. All rights reserved. Printed in Canada.**
The DALMATIAN PRESS name, logo, spotted spine and Tear and Share are trademarks of Dalmatian Press, LLC, Franklin, Tennessee 37067. No part of this book may be reproduced or copied in any form without written permission from the copyright owner.

03 04 05 06 QSR 10 9 8 7 6 5 4 3 2
12386/VEGGIETALES: Heroes of the Bible

Crossword Puzzle
Fill in the blanks to the VeggieTales theme song!

Know your Veggies!
(They're good for you!)

1 across   If you like to talk to _____ ,

2 down   If a _____ can make you smile,

3 across   If you like to waltz with _____ ,

3 down   Up and down the _____ aisle...

Have We Got a Show For You!

VeggieTales! VeggieTales!

VeggieTales! VeggieTales!

VeggieTales! VeggieTales!

VeggieTales! VeggieTales!

4 across   _____ . Celery. Gotta be... VeggieTales!

5 down   Lima beans. Collard _____ . Peachy keen! VeggieTales!

6 across   _____ . Sweet and sour. Half an hour. VeggieTales!

There's never, ever, ever, ever, ever been a show like VeggieTales!

There's never, ever, ever, ever, ever been a show like VeggieTales!

7 across   It's time for _____ !

ANSWERS: 1 ACROSS – TOMATOES, 2 DOWN – SQUASH, 3 ACROSS – POTATOES, 3 DOWN – PRODUCE, 4 ACROSS – BROCCOLI, 5 DOWN – GREENS, 6 ACROSS – CAULIFLOWER, 7 ACROSS – VEGGIETALES

Dalmatian Press

Rack, Shack and Benny

Stand firm and hold to the teachings we passed on to you.
— 2 Thessalonians 2:15

"I'm Rack!" "I'm Shack!" "I'm Benny!"
"We work hard at the Nezzer Chocolate Factory."

Dalmatian Press

Secret Code

Use the code to find out the boys' real names.

___	___	___	___	___	___	___	___
19	8	1	4	18	1	3	8

___	___	___	___	___	___	___
13	5	19	8	1	3	8

___	___	___	___	___	___	___	___
1	2	5	4	14	5	7	15

Code

1 = A
2 = B
3 = C
4 = D
5 = E
6 = F
7 = G
8 = H
9 = I
10 = J
11 = K
12 = L
13 = M
14 = N
15 = O
16 = P
17 = Q
18 = R
19 = S
20 = T
21 = U
22 = V
23 = W
24 = X
25 = Y
26 = Z

Of course, no one can remember those names, so we'll just call them:

RACK, SHACK and Benny.

"I'm Laura. I work at the factory.
We make chocolate bunnies for Mr. Nebby K. Nezzer."

"I love chocolate bunnies! Won't it be a beautiful thing when everybody bows down to my 90-foot bunny...

...while they sing the Bunny Song!"
The Bunny! The Bunny! Yeah, I love the bunny!
I just want a plate and a fork and a bunny!!

When it was time, everyone bowed down
and sang to Mr. Nezzer's Big Bunny...

...except Rack, Shack and Benny. They loved God.
They knew it was wrong to bow and sing to a bunny.

Dalmatian Press

Mr. Nezzer was furious. "Guards! Seize them!
Into the furnace with those bad bunnies!"

Back at the factory...
"Rack, I can't move my arms!"
"Uh, Benny, you don't have any arms."

Help Laura find her way to rescue the boys.

START

FINISH

Laura to the rescue! "Sorry, Mr. Nezzer!
Nobody bakes my buddies! Hang on, guys!"

The guards chased Laura as Rack, Shack and Benny
got closer to the fiery furnace!
Some guards fell — splat! — right into the chocolate!

"God will watch out for us!" said Shack.
And then our heroes fell into the fiery furnace!

But something strange happened. Light streamed into
the furnace, filling the factory with an eerie glow.

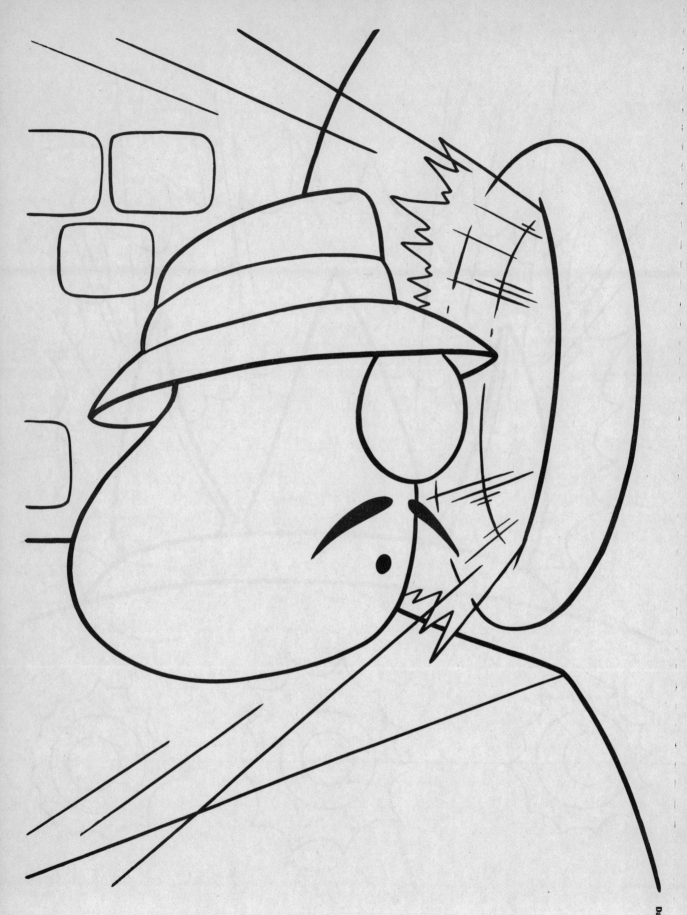

"Hey, boss. There are *four* guys in there now... and one
of them's real shiny! And they ain't burning up!"

"Rack! Shack! Benny! Come out of there!" cried Mr. Nezzer.
"God has saved you from the fiery furnace! Can you ever forgive me?"

"We forgive you," said Rack, Shack, and Benny.
If you stand up for what you believe in, God will stand with YOU!

DaNiEL iN THE Lions' Den

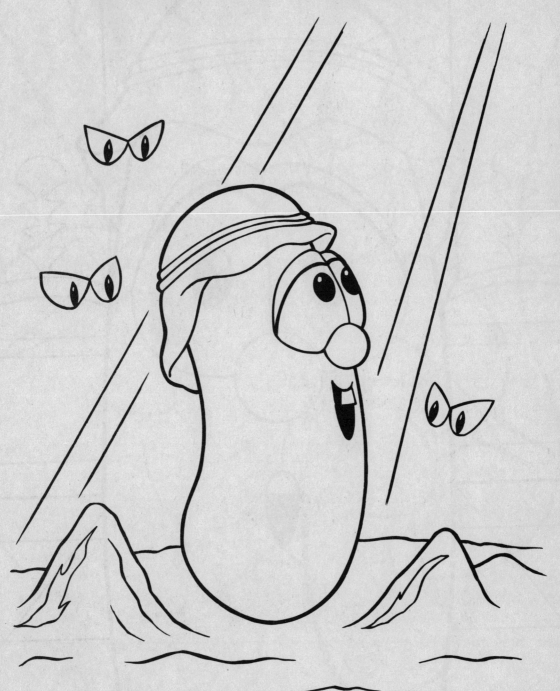

So do not fear, for I am with you.
—Isaiah 41:10

Long ago, the King of Babylon took young Daniel
to live in his city and go to school in his palace.

One morning, King Darius said to his wise men,
"I've had a dream! Someone tell me what it means!"

"We are wise, but not that wise," they said.
"Call Daniel. Perhaps he can explain."

WHICH DANIEL is DIFFERENT?

A

B

C

D

YOUR ANSWER:

ANSWER: B

With the wisdom God gave him, Daniel explained the dream.
This made the King so happy, he made Daniel his second in command!

Then the wise men had to obey Daniel. This made them unhappy!
"Oh, no! What're we gonna do?"

So the wise men tricked King Darius into passing a new law.
Now everyone must pray only to King Darius, or be eaten by lions.

LOOK UP, DOWN, ACROSS AND DIAGONALLY TO FIND WORDS FROM THE NEW LAW.

EVERYONE

PRAY

ONLY

KING

EATEN

LIONS

```
E A T E N Z A A P A P W F J
G W X L H X K I N G Q R B L
H D G E H B C J E S A D A H
U G I N F N G I Y A Y Y S Y
O H L O D M J U U Z T A E A
M O K Y S L M Y A F R Q T E
C L M R A S N T W V E B U T
S M J E R Y N R C H W N O E
A B H V Y R X O X M S M N R
L X T E I E Z W I K X K L Y
P Q R D P W A I N L C L Y M
```

Daniel understood the King's law, but he did not want to disobey God.
So, he still prayed to God. As he prayed, the wise men burst into his room!

Daniel broke the King's law, so they threw him in the lions' den!
"What am I gonna do? It looks like I'll end up as lion stew!"

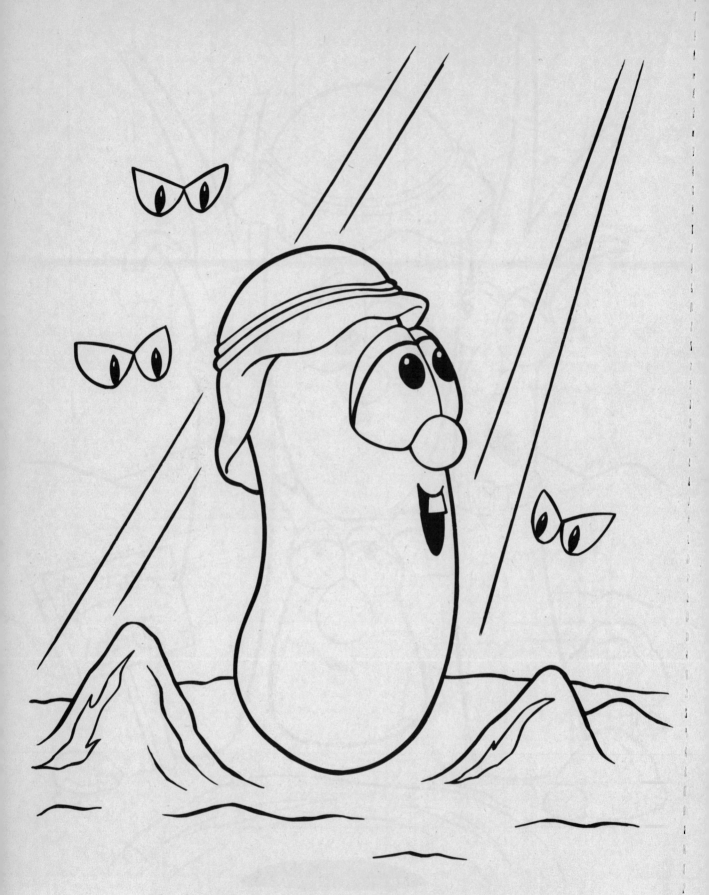

The darkness scared Daniel, until he heard an angel say,
"God hears your prayers."
Daniel trusted God, even though he was afraid.

The King knew he had lost a good friend, so he prayed
that Daniel's God would protect him.

The next morning, everyone ran to the lions' den.
The King was sad. "Nobody survives a night with lions!"

Dalmatian Press

But then there was a voice! *"Hello!!! Hellooooo!!!!"*

Secret Code

Use the code to find out how Daniel survived the lions' den.

$\overline{}$ $\overline{}$ $\overline{}$ $\overline{}$ $\overline{}$ $\overline{}$ $\overline{}$ $\overline{}$
8   5   16 18 1 25 5 4

$\overline{}$ $\overline{}$ $\overline{}$
1 14 4

$\overline{}$ $\overline{}$ $\overline{}$ $\overline{}$ $\overline{}$ $\overline{}$ $\overline{}$ $\overline{}$ $\overline{}$ $\overline{}$
20 18 21 19 20 5 4   7 15 4

Code

1 = A
2 = B
3 = C
4 = D
5 = E
6 = F
7 = G
8 = H
9 = I
10 = J
11 = K
12 = L
13 = M
14 = N
15 = O
16 = P
17 = Q
18 = R
19 = S
20 = T
21 = U
22 = V
23 = W
24 = X
25 = Y
26 = Z

"Goodbye! Thanks for the pizza!" Daniel called to the lions.
Everyone was amazed, especially the King.

Help Daniel get past the lions' den.

"From this day forth, everyone will pray only to Daniel's God*!!*"
the King ordered. "Forget this silly praying-to-me business.
Who's idea was that anyway?*!!*"

When they heard that, the wise men left as fast as they could!
But Daniel stayed. And God blessed him all his days.

Dave and the Giant Pickle

With God, all things are possible.
— Matthew 19:26

Long ago, a boy named David lived with his seven brothers
in a land called Israel. Mostly, they watched sheep.

Watching sheep was hard work, since their sheep had an unusual problem.
They'd tip over.

One day their dad, Jesse, came running out to the sheep-fields
with some horrible news! "The Philistines are attacking!"

So what's so bad about the Philistines, anyway?

Decode the words to find out!

Code

$\overline{20}$ $\overline{8}$ $\overline{5}$ $\overline{25}$ $\overline{23}$ $\overline{1}$ $\overline{14}$ $\overline{20}$

$\overline{20}$ $\overline{15}$ $\overline{19}$ $\overline{20}$ $\overline{5}$ $\overline{1}$ $\overline{12}$ $\overline{20}$ $\overline{8}$ $\overline{5}$

$\overline{12}$ $\overline{1}$ $\overline{14}$ $\overline{4}$ $\overline{15}$ $\overline{6}$ $\overline{9}$ $\overline{19}$ $\overline{18}$ $\overline{1}$ $\overline{5}$ $\overline{12}$

$\overline{6}$ $\overline{18}$ $\overline{15}$ $\overline{13}$ $\overline{20}$ $\overline{8}$ $\overline{5}$

$\overline{9}$ $\overline{19}$ $\overline{18}$ $\overline{1}$ $\overline{5}$ $\overline{12}$ $\overline{9}$ $\overline{20}$ $\overline{5}$ $\overline{19}$.

Code

1 = A
2 = B
3 = C
4 = D
5 = E
6 = F
7 = G
8 = H
9 = I
10 = J
11 = K
12 = L
13 = M
14 = N
15 = O
16 = P
17 = Q
18 = R
19 = S
20 = T
21 = U
22 = V
23 = W
24 = X
25 = Y
26 = Z

So the Philippines are bad guys!

No, the Philippines are islands in the Pacific Ocean. Philistines are bad guys!

ANSWER: THEY WANT TO STEAL THE LAND OF ISRAEL FROM THE ISRAELITES.

**King Saul was building an army to stop the Philistines.
"We must save Israel! We must save Israel!"**

"Hold on there, Dave," Jesse said. "You're a little guy.
Let the big guys go. You stay with the sheep."

The brothers found King Saul's camp, and the armies
were doing what they did back then — they yelled at each other.

Code

1 = A
2 = B
3 = C
4 = D
5 = E
6 = F
7 = G
8 = H
9 = I
10 = J
11 = K
12 = L
13 = M
14 = N
15 = O
16 = P
17 = Q
18 = R
19 = S
20 = T
21 = U
22 = V
23 = W
24 = X
25 = Y
26 = Z

So what were the Philistines yelling?

_____

They wanted the Israelites to be their slaves, because they could force slaves to:

_____

__ __ __ __ __   __ __ __
6 5 20 3 8   20 8 5

__ __ __ __ __ __ __ __ __ __ __ ,
1 14 14 1 14 14 14 14 1 14 14

__ __ __ __ __ __ __ __ !
7 15 4 7 15 4 15 4

DECODE THE WORDS
TO FIND OUT WHAT SLAVES
WOULD HAVE TO DO.

ANSWER: FETCH THE PHILISTINES' SLIPPERS!

Everyone got tired of the yelling, and the Philistines seemed... small!
So King Saul agreed to a fight between champions.
"Send out your champion!"

"Whom will I fight!?" Goliath roared.
The Israelites were so scared that they all ran away and hid!

Jesse sent little Dave with some food for his brothers.
When Dave arrived, Goliath was still waiting for someone to fight!

Which Goliath is Different?

ANSWER: D

"No one to fight," Goliath mumbled.
"You're not God's children! You are cowards!"
That was too much for Dave! SOMEONE had to fight Goliath!

King Saul couldn't believe his ears! And his armor wasn't much help.
But Dave had courage, so he let him fight Goliath.

"I come in the name of God who will help me defeat you!" said Dave.
That made Goliath really mad! Then Dave put a rock in his sling...

UNSCRAMBLE

1. Who attacked the Israelites?

iLiSTineSPH 　（O）＿ ＿ ＿ ＿ ＿ ＿ ＿ ＿ ＿ ＿

2. What does Dave need to fight Goliath?

GECOURA 　＿ ＿ （O）＿ ＿ ＿ ＿ ＿

3. What tips over a lot at Dave's home?

eeSHP 　（O）＿ ＿ ＿ ＿

4. How many brothers does Dave have?

venSe 　（O）＿ ＿ ＿ ＿

5. Who is the champion for the Philistines?

GOiaTHL 　＿ ＿ ＿ （O）＿ ＿ ＿

6. Goliath is:

iGB 　（O）＿ ＿

7. Dave is:

LeTLiT 　＿ ＿ ＿ ＿ （O）＿

8. A little guy who can do big things with God's help.

VeaD 　＿ ＿ ＿ （O）

Read down the circled letters to finish this verse:
"With God, all things are ＿＿＿＿＿＿＿." —Matthew 19:26

ANSWERS: 1. PHILISTINES, 2. COURAGE, 3. SHEEP, 4. SEVEN, 5. GOLIATH, 6. BIG, 7. LITTLE, 8. DAVE

Everyone watched as the scary Philistine giant wiggled, then wobbled...
then fell over! When the Philistines saw that, they all ran away and hid!

Israel was saved!

So that's the story of Dave, a really little guy,
who — with God's help — did a really big thing!

JOSH AND THE BIG WALL

As for God, His way is perfect. — 2 Samuel 22:31a

This is Joshua. God chose Joshua
to lead the Israelites after Moses died.

After forty years in the desert, the Israelites were ready
to follow God. So Joshua led them to the Promised Land!

"It'll be so great! Oh, we can hardly wait!
Because we're goin' to the Promised Land!"

Help the Israelites find their way from Egypt to the Promised Land.

Egypt

START

FINISH

Land of Milk and Honey

So off they went as Joshua led them to the Promised Land.
Unfortunately, there was a problem...

Jericho!

"Someone has bumped our wall!
Who are you?" asked the soldiers of Jericho.

"I am Joshua. And these are the children of Israel!" Joshua told them.
"Oh, hello, children!" said the soldiers. "Now, go away!"

"You don't understand," Joshua explained. "God has given us this land for our new home. So... *you're* the ones who have to leave."

"Ho-ho-ho!" laughed the soldiers. "We'd like to see you try to get over our wall, tiny pickle!!"

"I'm a cucumber," Joshua told them, as a slushee fell off the wall and landed right on top of one of the Israelites.

The Israelites decided to go talk things over.
"Maybe we should go back to Egypt," said Pa Grape.

"Jerry and I are going to come up with a plan
to take out that wall!" declared Jimmy.

Joshua decided to go off by himself to talk to God.
Suddenly, he saw a strange man...

...who said, "I am the commander of the army of the LORD."
Josh fell face down on the ground in reverence.

"I come with directions from the LORD!"
"I am the LORD's servant," said Joshua.

THE LORD'S DIRECTIONS

The LORD says to you: "See, Joshua! I have delivered **Jericho** into your hands! **March** around the city once with all your men. Do this each day for six days! Have seven **priests** carry **trumpets** of ram horns in front of the ark. On the seventh day, march around the city **seven** times, with the priests blowing the trumpets! When you hear them sound a long blast, have all the people give a loud **shout**, and the **walls** of the city will collapse and Jericho will be yours!!"

LOOK UP, DOWN, ACROSS AND DIAGONALLY TO FIND THESE WORDS.

JERICHO **PRIESTS** **SEVEN**

WALLS

MARCH **TRUMPETS** **SHOUT**

```
A K J I F Z Q O V A P W M Q
W A L L S L A H C L J K J A
D H B B H K S C D O K I U X
T Y F H U P R I E S T S Y Z
R G G J I J S R W H E P T R
U B T N O U G E R Y S T G T
M V Q M R N H J V G A R B T
P F W A E Y I D J E Q E U O
E C C R D B K S U F N O R P
T D K C S G P Q I V H A F K
S X P H A V L A O S C Q S L
```

Joshua went back to camp and told God's directions.
"That might work if the walls were made of Jello," said Jimmy.

"Last call for Egypt!" cried Pa Grape.
"Who's comin' with me?"

"Blowing horns in the desert just isn't gonna do it.
What we need is serious firepower!" Jimmy told them.

Then Jerry removed a large curtain to reveal their new creation. "Behold! The Wall-minator 3000!"

"Um... We should try God's way first. He'll take care of us," said Joshua.
So the Israelites agreed to follow God's directions...

...and the next morning, there they were —
marching around Jericho.

"Keep walking! But you won't knock down our wall!
Keep walking! But it isn't gonna fall!"

The soldiers threw down their slushees at the Israelites.
But that didn't stop them! They made it all the way around Jericho.

WHICH GUARD SLUSHEED THE GOURD?

ANSWER: C

Back at their camp that night, Josh said,
"That could have been worse! We only have to do this six more days!"

Dalmatian Press

"I've got slushee in my ear! Let's fire up the Wall-minator, Jerry!"
"Anyone want to head back to Egypt with me?" asked Pa Grape.

"Wait!" cried Junior. "Remember what happened when we didn't follow God's directions? God's way is always the best way!"

"Let's go to Jericho!" they all cheered.
It wasn't easy, but they marched around Jericho — for six more days.

On the seventh day, the Israelites did exactly what God had
told them to do. Then they all yelled!

At first nothing happened. Then, the walls fell apart
and the towers collapsed — just as God had promised!

"Hello! My name is Joshua,
and God has given us this land!"

The Israelites had finally obeyed God,
and God provided them with a new home.
This was a very happy day, indeed!

Secret Code
Use the code to find a very important message!

$\overline{}$ $\overline{}$ $\overline{}$ $\overline{}$ $\overline{}$ $\overline{}$ $\overline{}$
7   15   4   13   1   4   5

25 15 21   19 16 5 3 9 1 12

1 14 4   8 5

12 15 22 5 19   25 15 21

22 5 18 25   13 21 3 8 !

Code

1 = A
2 = B
3 = C
4 = D
5 = E
6 = F
7 = G
8 = H
9 = I
10 = J
11 = K
12 = L
13 = M
14 = N
15 = O
16 = P
17 = Q
18 = R
19 = S
20 = T
21 = U
22 = V
23 = W
24 = X
25 = Y
26 = Z

ANSWER: GOD MADE YOU SPECIAL AND HE LOVES YOU VERY MUCH!